HAL•LEONARD

INSTRUMENTAL
PLAY-ALONG

AUDIO
ACCESS
INCLUDED

VIOLIN

JAMES BOND

PLAYBACK+
Speed • Pitch • Balance • Loop

To access audio visit:
www.halleonard.com/mylibrary

Enter Code
7820-5057-5932-6738

Audio arrangements by Peter Deneff

ISBN 978-1-4950-6085-4

 **Music Sales America**

EXCLUSIVELY DISTRIBUTED BY

 HAL•LEONARD®

7777 W. BLUEMOUND RD. P.O. BOX 13819 MILWAUKEE, WI 53213

Visit Hal Leonard Online at
www.halleonard.com

DIAMONDS ARE FOREVER

from DIAMONDS ARE FOREVER

VIOLIN

Words by DON BLACK
Music by JOHN BARRY

FOR YOUR EYES ONLY

from FOR YOUR EYES ONLY

VIOLIN

Lyrics by MICHAEL LESSON
Music by BILL CONTI

FROM RUSSIA WITH LOVE

from FROM RUSSIA WITH LOVE

VIOLIN

Words and Music by
LIONEL BART

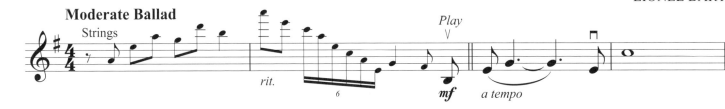

GOLDFINGER

from GOLDFINGER

VIOLIN

Music by JOHN BARRY
Lyrics by LESLIE BRICUSSE and ANTHONY NEWLEY

JAMES BOND THEME

VIOLIN

By MONTY NORMAN

LIVE AND LET DIE

from LIVE AND LET DIE

VIOLIN

Words and Music by PAUL McCARTNEY
and LINDA McCARTNEY

Slow Ballad

NOBODY DOES IT BETTER

from THE SPY WHO LOVED ME

VIOLIN

Music by MARVIN HAMLISCH
Lyrics by CAROLE BAYER SAGER

ON HER MAJESTY'S SECRET SERVICE - THEME

VIOLIN

By JOHN BARRY

SKYFALL
from the Motion Picture SKYFALL

VIOLIN

Words and Music by ADELE ADKINS
and PAUL EPWORTH

Slowly, with feeling

A VIEW TO A KILL
from A VIEW TO A KILL

VIOLIN

Words and Music by JOHN BARRY
and DURAN DURAN

WRITING'S ON THE WALL

from the film SPECTRE

VIOLIN

Words and Music by SAM SMITH
and JAMES NAPIER

YOU ONLY LIVE TWICE

from YOU ONLY LIVE TWICE

VIOLIN

Music by JOHN BARRY
Lyrics by LESLIE BRICUSSE